DATE DUE		

Science Links

Wildfires

Susan Ring

CHELSEA
CLUBHOUSE

An Imprint of Chelsea House Publishers

A Haights Cross Communications Company

Philadelphia

This edition first published in 2003 by Chelsea Clubhouse, a division of
Chelsea House Publishers and a subsidiary of Haights Cross Communications.

A Haights Cross Communications Company

This edition was adapted from Newbridge Discovery Links® by arrangement with Newbridge Educational Publishing.
All rights reserved. No part of this publication may be reproduced or transmitted in any form or by any means without
the written permission of the publisher. Printed and bound in the United States of America.

Chelsea Clubhouse
1974 Sproul Road, Suite 400
Broomall, PA 19008-0914

The Chelsea House world wide web address is www.chelseahouse.com

Library of Congress Cataloging-in-Publication Data
Ring, Susan.
  Wildfires / by Susan Ring.
     p. cm. — (Science links)
Contents: Fire! — Fighting wildfires — Can fires be good? — Keeping the balance.
  ISBN 0-7910-7432-3
  1. Wildfires—Juvenile literature. 2. Forest fires—Juvenile literature. 3. Fire ecology—Juvenile literature. [1. Wildfires. 2.
Forest fires. 3. Fire ecology. 4. Ecology.] I. Title. II. Series.
  SD421.23 .R56 2003
  363.37'9—dc21
                                                                                              2002015890

Newbridge Discovery Links Guided Reading Program Author: Dr. Brenda Parkes
Content Reviewer: Dr. Philip N. Omi, Western Forest Fire Research Center (WESTFIRE),
Colorado State University, Fort Collins, CO
Written by Susan Ring

Photo Credits:
Cover: Courtesy of the Bureau of Land Management; Table of Contents page: Joel Sartone/CORBIS; pages 4-5:
Courtesy of the Bureau of Land Management; page 6: Gary Wither/Bruce Coleman Photography, Inc.; page 7: Joel
Sartone/CORBIS; pages 8-9: Courtesy of the Bureau of Land Management; page 10: Raymond Gehman/CORBIS;
page 11: Courtesy of the Bureau of Land Management; page 12: Richard R. Hansen/Photo Researchers; page 13:
Reuters NewMedia, Inc./CORBIS; page 14: Courtesy of the Bureau of Land Management; page 15: (top) Raymond
Gehman/CORBIS, (bottom) Karen Wattenmaker/911 Pictures; page 16: Courtesy of the Bureau of Land Management;
page 17: Kevin R. Morris/CORBIS; page 18: Dave Bartuff/Index Stock, (inset) William R Hewlett/California Academy
of Sciences; page 19: Raymond Gehman/CORBIS; page 20: (top) Wolfgang Kaehler/CORBIS, (right) Karen
Wattenmaker/911 Pictures, (bottom) Phil A. Dotson/Photo Researchers, (left) Scott T. Smith/CORBIS; page 21: Georg
Gerster/Photo Researchers; page 22: Erwin and Peggy Bauer/Bruce Coleman, Inc.

While every care has been taken to trace and acknowledge photo copyrights for this edition, the publisher apologizes
for any accidental infringement where copyright has proved untraceable.

Table of Contents

Fire!

A weather satellite picture taken at the beginning of August 2000 showed a gray cloudy haze covering hundreds of miles of land across Idaho and Montana. But the gray haze wasn't rain clouds. August is wildfire season in the western United States, and the haze was smoke coming from raging wildfires.

A month earlier, lightning started one of the first large fires of the season in Clear Creek, Idaho. The fire burned for more than 90 days and blackened almost 200,000 acres (81,000 hectares) of land.

Soon after, wildfires tearing through the Bitterroot Valley in Montana consumed more than 300,000 acres (121,000 hectares) of land. By the end of September, more than 100 wild-fires had spread over Montana and Idaho, burn-ing an area of land larger than Rhode Island.

What causes such massive wildfires?

Temperatures from a wildfire can reach 1000 degrees Fahrenheit (538 degrees celcius), with flames shooting more than 300 feet (91 meters) into the air.

What Is a Wildfire?

Wildfires can break out anywhere. They can roar through the dense forests of Montana or Wyoming. They can sweep through the brushland of southern California. They can race across the prairies in Nebraska. Wildfires can hit any natural or **wildland** area.

Ingredients Every Fire Needs

A wildfire—just like any fire—needs three things in order to burn.

1. Heat: Lightning, a burning match, and coals from a campfire are all sources of heat that cause wildfires.

2. Oxygen: Oxygen is in the air we breathe. Water puts out fires because the water will not let oxygen get to the fire. It also reduces the heat.

3. Fuel: Trees and shrubs act as the fire's fuel.

Dry weather and little rain increase the possibility of wildfires' breaking out. Most wildfires take place during an area's dry season.

Many wildfires are caused by humans, but some are natural fires started by lightning. Any fire spreading too quickly across dry, parched land or threatening homes and communities near the edge of a wildland area is called a wildfire and needs to be stopped.

Fighting Wildfires

A wildfire can start in a remote part of a national park or forest, miles away from roads or trails. It can spread over thousands of acres of wilderness. How do firefighters battle these enormous fires? Fighting wildfires requires specially trained teams of firefighters, called **wildland firefighters**, and the right equipment for the job.

Perfect aim is an essential skill for smoke jumpers. They must avoid rivers, jagged rocks, cliffs, and the fire, when they parachute onto the scene.

Smoke jumpers are one of the first teams brought in to fight a wildfire. They are part of what is called the **initial attack**.

Smoke jumpers fight wildfires in places far from highways or other roads. Teams of smoke jumpers are flown to the site. Then they find a spot where they can land safely and parachute down. This is the quickest way to get firefighters to a fire.

Hotshot crews are also part of the initial attack. These experienced teams of firefighters hike or travel by truck to the most dangerous parts of the fire. **Hand crews**, teams of about 20 people, are also sent in to fight wildfires.

Once they are on the scene, wildland firefighters begin to dig a **fire line**. Using chain saws, shovels, axes, and other tools, the firefighters clear away the trees, shrubs, and **litter** that cover the forest floor to make a wide path. Fire lines can be anywhere from 2 feet (61 centimeters) to 200 feet (61 meters) wide and run for miles through a wildland area.

Wildland firefighters carry with them all the supplies they need, including food and water. They can spend days in the field fighting a fire.

Smoke jumpers and hotshot crews may be called in from across the country to fight a large wildfire.

The fire line helps stop the fire from spreading. When flames reach a fire line, they run out of fuel.

Another way firefighters stop wildfires is by setting fires! The firefighters start a **backfire**, which burns up a stretch of land in front of the fire. The backfire consumes all the trees, shrubs, and litter that can fuel the fire. It's a way for firefighters to extend a fire line and slow the spread of a fire.

A pink dye is added to the fire retardant. This helps the pilot to see where it lands.

Flying Fire Engines

Also on hand are fleets of helicopters and planes that can attack the fire from the sky.

Helicopters are brought in for bucket drops. A huge bucket, which dangles from the bottom of the helicopter, scoops up water from a nearby lake or river. Then the helicopter ferries the bucket to a fire's hot spot and douses it with as much as 300 gallons (1,136 liters) of water.

Firefighting planes called **airtankers** can spray a line of water or **fire retardant** around a fire to stop it from spreading. Airtankers can transport as much as 3,000 gallons (11,356 liters).

The Command Center

Workers at the fire command center monitor both the crews working in the field and all the equipment used to fight the fire. They track the fire's movement and develop a plan to contain the fire.

The command center also stays in touch with the National Weather Service. Knowing whether the wind will switch direction or whether there is rain in the forecast is very important for fighting fires.

Helicopters can deliver water to wildfires burning far from roads. Helicopters are also used to bring in supplies, food, and firefighters.

Tools of the Trade

Wildland firefighters wear protective clothing and use tools designed just for combating wildfires. The tools must be lightweight but very strong. What tools and equipment do you think wildland firefighters need?

Fire-resistant pants and shirts help keep firefighters safe. Goggles, gloves, helmets, and leather boots are also worn for safety. Every firefighter carries a **fire shelter**, too. This small tent made of fireproof material protects firefighters from heat and smoke if they are trapped too close to a fire.

Three tools a firefighter uses:

- A combination ax and digging tool called a **Pulaski**
- A heavy duty tool called a **McLeod** that works like a rake and a hoe
- A shovel with sharpened edges that can cut through roots and undergrowth

Why do you think each tool is designed to do more than one job?

What does it take to become a wildland firefighter?

Firefighters must pass a pack test, which means completing a 3-mile (4.8-kilometer) hike in less than 45 minutes while carrying a 45-pound (20.4-kilogram) pack.

After the fire is out, firefighters go in for the **mop-up**. This is the time they check for "hot spots," small areas that are still burning. Some firefighters use a backpack pump, which is filled with water, to cool down the hot spots.

Can Fires Be Good?

After a fire sweeps through an area, the ground is black and covered with ash. But even though the land looks devastated, some fires are actually good for forests and other wildland areas.

Lightning has started fires in the wilderness for thousands of years. These fires are part of the natural **cycle** of growth in the wild. Fire is almost as important to many environments as sunlight and rain.

Deer, wolves, bears, and other large animals can usually escape from a wildfire. After the fire, predators like wolves and coyotes will feast on the small animals that have been left homeless by the fire.

Plants quickly return after even the most devastating fire.

Nature's Recycling Plan

Natural fires clear a forest floor of decomposing leaves, branches, and other dead matter on the ground.

The ashes that remain put nutrients back into the soil. This makes the soil even better for the new trees and bushes that will grow.

Fire also clears the way for more sunlight to reach the forest floor. The sunlight helps the new plants and trees to grow.

Fireproof Plants

Many of the trees and plants that thrive in forests, prairies, and other wildland areas have adapted to fires. There are trees that have fire-resistant bark, plants that grow back very quickly after a fire, and even some plants that grow only after a fire. Their seedpods need the heat of the fire in order to pop open. These plants and trees can grow back stronger than ever after a fire.

Shrub oak, ceanothus, and other plants that grow in the brushland burn quickly during a fire. But they can also sprout and grow back very quickly.

Native plants such as Indian grass and bluestem grow in tallgrass prairies. These plants provide food and nesting areas for many types of animals.

Keeping Out Intruders

A natural fire prevents non-native plants and trees from invading and taking over an area. Without natural fires, the tallgrass prairies in Nebraska, Kansas, and other parts of the midwestern United States would disappear. Larger shrubs and trees would take root, then spread across the prairie.

Lodgepole Pines

If it weren't for forest fires, the lodgepole pines wouldn't exist today. Lodgepole pines are tall pine trees that grow in the western part of the United States.

Lodgepole pines grow tall and create shade. Fir and spruce trees grow in this shade. But new lodgepole pines cannot replace the old and dying lodgepoles. New lodgepole pines can't grow in the shade.

Fire also clears the forest floor and thins out the trees in the forest. This helps sunlight reach the forest floor. New lodgepole pine seedlings can get the sunshine they need to grow.

Heat from a fire causes the lodgepole seeds to burst from their cones. Their cones open only at very high temperatures — between 113°F and 140°F (45° and 60° C).

Keeping the Balance

In the past, people believed that any wildfire was bad. They didn't realize that natural fires were good for forests and other wildland areas. So every fire was put out. But that interrupted the forest's natural cycle.

Forests grew very thick with more trees and more undergrowth. Dense trees and too much undergrowth result in more fuel to burn—and that can be dangerous. Natural fires can quickly turn into wildfires burning out of control.

The forest service sometimes starts small, controlled fires. Burning old, dry undergrowth helps prevent major fires. A fire ecologist must carefully study a wilderness area before deciding whether to set a fire.

MORTAR CR. FIRE
--- Fire Boundary 8-8-79 (0100
--- Fire Boundary 8-9-79 (0100
○ Fire Boundary & Hot Spots
8-10-79 (0100
○ Fire Boundary & Hot Spots
8-11-79 (0100
Total of 61,140 Acres

MORTAR CR. FIRE
~ Fire Boundary 8-9-79 (0100)
--- Fire Boundary 8-10-79 (0100)
○ Fire Boundary 8-10-79 (0100)
○ Fire Boundary 8-11-79 (0100)
61,140 Acres

Today, **fire ecologists** have learned to let natural fires burn themselves out. This preserves the natural cycle of fire and regrowth that can keep natural environments healthy. It also prevents larger fires from turning into devastating wildfires.

Forests and other wildland areas don't stay the same. Just like any living thing, they grow and change. And fires are a very important part of that cycle.

Natural fires can help renew a forest area like this one.

Glossary

airtanker: a plane that sprays water or fire retardant on a wildfire

backfire: a fire started by firefighters in order to stop or contain a fire

cycle: events or a series of events that are repeated over and over again, as in the natural cycle of growth, fire, and regrowth in a forest

fire ecologists: scientists who study wildfires and the role of fire in natural environments

fire line: a strip of land that has been cleared of trees, shrubs, and other flammable materials in order to stop a fire from spreading

fire shelter: a special tent that protects firefighters from smoke and flames if a fire gets too close

fire retardant: a substance that slows or stops the spread of a fire

hand crews: teams of wildland firefighters

hotshot crews: specially trained teams of wildland firefighters

initial attack: the first attempt to stop or extinguish a wildfire

litter: the dead leaves, pine needles, branches, and other materials that cover the ground in a forest or other wildland area

McLeod: a firefighting tool that is a combination of a rake and a hoe

mop-up: the cleanup after a wildfire, during which time firefighters check to make sure the fire is completely out

Pulaski: a firefighting tool that is a combination of an ax and a digging tool

smoke jumpers: wildland firefighters who parachute into an area to fight a wildfire

wildland: forest, grassland, brushland, or other uncultivated land

wildland firefighter: firefighters who battle fires in forests, grasslands, brushlands, or other wildland areas

Index

Websites

Learn more about wildfires by visiting these Websites:

www.fema.gov/kids/wldfire.htm

www.smokeybear.com

www.infoplease.com/spot/forestfire1.html